BETWEEN THE FENCES

BETWEEN THE FENCES

An
Autobiography By:

FRED THOMPSON

DJs Legacy Publishing House

DJs legacy incorporated

CONTENTS

I Fred Thompson , Dedicate this book "Between The Fences" , To my Family, Friends , & Most of all God!

CHAPTER 1

Overcoming Adversity

In the annals of history, there have been countless tales of individuals who, despite facing insurmountable challenges, managed to rise above adversity and leave an indelible mark on the world. One such extraordinary journey is that of Fred Thompson, a young man born on July 6th,1927 in Little Nowata,Oklahoma. Along with his sister, shared a profound love for their parents, Jesse Thompson and Jessie Alcock. This biography dives into the life of Fred Thompson, tracing his path as he navigated through a world marred by racism, personal hardships, and the tumultuous times of war. Through his unwavering love for his family and his remarkable resilience, Thompson's story serves as a testament to the power of the human spirit to triumph over life's most daunting challenges.

CHAPTER 2

A Childhood Marked by Racism

Fred Thompson's journey began in a time when racism and discrimination were still deeply ingrained in society. As a young boy, he witnessed firsthand the painful consequences of prejudice, as his opportunities for education and personal growth were consistently hindered. Despite his intellectual prowess and thirst for knowledge, Fred Thompson was denied the chance to graduate, solely because of the color of his skin. It was during these formative years that he first learned the importance of perseverance and the significance of standing up against injustice. In addition to the adversity Fred Thompson faced due to racism, he was burdened with the responsibility of caring for his sickly parents, Jesse Thompson and Jessie Alcock. As their only son, he shouldered the weight of their deteriorating health, sacrificing his own aspirations for the sake of their well-being. The love he harbored for his parents propelled him forward, providing him with the strength to endure the challenges that lay ahead. Jesse's unwavering dedication to his family serves as a reminder of the profound impact familial love can have on shaping one's destiny.

CHAPTER 3

The Call to Serve

Drafted into War As fate would have it, Fred Thompson's journey took an unexpected turn when he was drafted into the war. The conflict thrust him into a world of violence and uncertainty, forcing him to confront the harsh realities of battle. Despite the fear and anguish that accompanied his deployment, Fred's unwavering love for his family propelled him forward, serving as a beacon of hope amidst the chaos. His experiences in war solidified his resolve to create a better world, free from the shackles of prejudice and discrimination.

CHAPTER 4

Triumph Over Adversity

A Life of Inspiration having emerged from the crucible of war, Thompson's resilience and determination continued to shape his life. He refused to succumb to the bitterness that often accompanies such hardships, instead choosing to channel his energy into positive change. Fred became a beacon of hope within his community, advocating for equality, and fighting against the very racism that had plagued his own upbringing. Through his acts of love, compassion, and unwavering dedication to his family, most of all his loving Wife Ethal, who's personal sacrifices helped push Thompson's journey serves as a testament to the transformative power of the human spirit.

CHAPTER 5

Has the hard work paid off?

Fred Thompson's journey from a young boy facing racism, to a devoted son caring for his sickly parents, and ultimately a soldier fighting in the war, is a testament to the resilience of the human spirit. Despite the trials he endured, Fred's love for his family remained the guiding force that propelled him forward. His unwavering determination to overcome adversity and create a better world is a source of inspiration for all who encounter his story. Thompson's remarkable journey serves as a poignant reminder that love, resilience, and a fervent belief in the power of change can overcome even the most daunting obstacles. This has been such a long journey, but God oh mighty has the hard work paid off!

In the annals of history, there have been countless tales of individuals who, despite facing insurmountable challenges, managed to rise above adversity and leave an indelible mark on the world.

www.ingramcontent.com/pod-product-compliance
Lightning Source LLC
Chambersburg PA
CBHW070330160726
47999CB00003B/1236